ANCHOR
BOOKS

TREASURE EACH MOMENT

Edited by

Heather Killingray

First published in Great Britain in 2002 by
ANCHOR BOOKS
Remus House,
Coltsfoot Drive,
Peterborough, PE2 9JX
Telephone (01733) 898102

HB ISBN 1 84418 051 4
SB ISBN 1 84418 052 2

FOREWORD

Anchor Books is a small press, established in 1992, with the aim of promoting readable poetry to as wide an audience as possible.

We hope to establish an outlet for writers of poetry who may have struggled to see their work in print.

The poems presented here have been selected from many entries, and as always editing proved to be a difficult task.

I trust this selection will delight and please the authors and all those who enjoy reading poetry.

Heather Killingray
Editor

CONTENTS

THAT SCRUFFY OLD BAG

That scruffy old bag
With everything in it
You knew what was there
Without looking in it

Your papers so neatly in envelopes sit
You could find 'whatever' without any hitch

Bandages, ointments - all now forsaken
Your bottles of tablets no more to be taken

Your comb and your brush no more to be used
Sitting beside one of your shoes
In that scruffy old bag which is our Mother's
That *she* needs no more - which *she* left with others

That scruffy old bag with pencils and pens
Memories linger with all of these things
Of a wonderful, caring and loveable Mother
Who has been taken from us forever and ever

God bless you and keep you in His Heavenly Parks
Where we'll meet once again when our journey starts.

Janet Carter

THE HARDEST THING

They say she was 'very comfortable',
The morning that she died,
She certainly seemed to be pain-free
I know, for I was at her side.

She didn't want to be alone,
She told us weeks before,
And I had promised to be there,
As she passed through that final door.

For ten long weeks the nurses cared,
They turned her, washed and fed,
Until her wasted body could move no more,
Imprisoned, motionless in a hospital bed.

She had been ill for as long as I remembered,
Always frail and weak,
But those last ten weeks were hell on earth,
As the illness reached its peak.

She didn't speak the last seven days,
But she knew that we were there,
And so we sat and held her hand
And told her that we cared.

They rang on Wednesday and said 'You'd better come,'
They rang Thursday as well,
'We thought it was the end' they said,
But you can never really tell.

It was still dark on Friday morning
When the final call came for me,
The night staff were waiting at the door,
With toast, and a cup of tea!

I said I couldn't swallow,
They said 'It won't be long
And you must look after yourself as well,
She needs you to be strong.'

I held her hand one last time,
And said just how much we cared,
I'll never be sure if she could hear
But I pray she knew I was there.

And, as finally, the pain lifted,
And I felt myself begin to cry,
I knew the hardest thing I'd ever done,
Was to watch my mother die.

Celia Parker

FRIENDSHIP

(Dedicated to Jean Geran, a special friend and workmate)

Our friendship grew over time,
Some views not like mine.
But that's what makes
friends special.
That's why we're good on
ward 11.

I'd like this friendship,
To last forever.
So in my heart,
We will be together.

I never knew you really cared,
I know this may sound absurd.
When you hugged me and,
Said goodbye,
What you did was make me cry.

So friends we have become,
Why couldn't I have
Someone like you for a *mum.*

S Christian

NAN

We arrived at Nan's.
Our visit was about once a week.
My nan's name was Elizabeth, but everyone called her Liz.
I embroidered for her a fish made of felt. On it was the name 'Nan'.
It made her smile.
Her hair was dark brown, she looked like a gypsy, with it tied
back in a scarf.
We were sent in the kitchen, my brother and I, to make some tea.
We looked in the cupboard to find the tea caddy.
To us the cupboard was magical.
It was called a larder.
There were matches, a tin of red salmon, which she kept for best,
A box of tea and all the rest.
You could walk in this cupboard.
To me it was heaven.
It was safe, it captured time.
I loved this cupboard.
To me it was Nan.

Elaine Backham

MY DAD, MY HERO

It still seems like a dream to me,
My dad, my hero, no more to be.
My whole world fell apart,
A tiny child with a broken heart.

25 years ago you went away,
Yet I still miss you every day.
It doesn't get easier as time goes on,
There's just more things that need to be done.

You were as near to perfect as there could be,
No one's ever come close, well, not to me!
As long as I'm alive, your memory will live on,
And then in my children after I've gone.

If I have to wait a lifetime, this I can bear,
If I know when I come, you'll be waiting there.
In the meantime, Dad, before I turn out the light,
I'll look at your photo, smile, and kiss you goodnight.

Elizabeth Kenworthy

MY LOVED ONES, I LOVE YOU

I'm going to tell our love story and how I think the world of you
You are my friend, my lover, and my greatest confidante too
You're my rock, my anchor and I need you by my side
Without you I would perish in life's fast-flowing tide
You gave me six lovely children, the most precious gift of all
Three beautiful, graceful girls, 'the three boys' are handsome and tall
I love each one dearly, more than they will ever know
I am sure they love me too, no need to tell me so
Life wasn't always easy, you worked hard and guided me through
In spite of opposition, you stood firm and loyal by me too
I thank you for your love all through our married life
I'm proud and happy you chose me to be your loving wife.

Angela Moore

A SON'S BEDROOM - WITH APOLOGIES TO WILLIAM SHAKESPEARE

'Shall I compare thee to a summer's day . . .'

Shall I compare thee to the common swine
Who rests supine within his filthy sty?
Hard words do trickle off thy lowly back
And unkind thoughts do naught but make me cry.
Sometime I gaze upon thy messy room,
And often is the golden carpet dimm'd
By clothes and books and cups of tea left there,
By papers, work, or football boots, untrimm'd.
But thy eternal chaos shall not fade
Nor lose possession of the things thou own'st;
Nor shalt thou brag thou searchest not in vain
Thou may'st be messy, but at least thou'rt honest.
    So long as men can breathe or eyes can see,
    So long lives mess, and this gives grief to me.

Liz Piper

SHALL I COMPARE THEE . . .?

*(I have written this as if it were my husband
writing about me)*

Shall I compare thee to a Range Rover
With four-wheel drive to run swift as the breeze?
Shall I dream of thee clothed silver over
With deep throttled voice roaring Lionese?

Sometime cruising along the ribbon road
Others bumping over the rocky scree;
Springs bouncing, sturdily taking the load;
Engine singing joyfully to be free.

But thy love mine heart, if it be mine true
Shall ride upon your beige leather seating,
In warmth and joy through life's journey with you.
Coveting your luxurious heating.

My hands shall caress your many features
And shall possess the fairest of creatures.

V M McKinley

LULLABY

Sleep well now little Bossy Boots
For time has slipped away
You will need to build up your strength
To boss them round next day

Sleep well my sweet petunia
Drooping little flower
You need to have your velvet voice
Charged up to full power

For where you play are naughty kids
You need to take in hand
As Xena Princess Warrior
You need to take command

For now it's just the nursery
Enough for one small girl
Next year it is the Isle of Man
And then perhaps the world!

So what if parents do complain
About our small cherub?
For little do they realise
Grandad's Beelzebub

John Smurthwaite

TEDDY BY NAME AND NATURE

The little man in my life is called Teddy.
Teddy by name and nature.

We spend all our time together,
Sometimes separated as Teddy is still young.

Tea parties, singing groups, swimming,
Play groups, library and long hot walks.
We attend all willing.

We both live on fizzy pop and cuddles.

Who is my teddy,
But my dear Son.

Parveen K Saini

ABOUT ME

How I feel about me?
Well that's not easy you see.
I can't write this in a letter,
But in a poem, now that's better

Sometimes I feel happy or sad,
Sometimes I feel angry or bad.
Sometimes I feel I'm going crazy,
Sometimes I feel I should be more brainy.

Why is it I feel pretty
Until I look in the mirror
And see me looking unpretty,
Then I start to feel bitter.

In my dreams I'm so pretty,
I have a beautiful figure.
In my dreams I'm so brainy,
That I pass all my exams and have a degree.

I also look at my life,
What I've done, where I've been.
Maybe it ain't such a bad life,
I think, I hope I ain't been really mean.

Now I have a nice new home
And a new love in my life.
My first-born son, and now I'm not alone,
Maybe this time I'll get my life right

Joanne Mills

GOODBYE QUEEN MOTHER

Today is such a very sad day,
Our dear Queen Mother has passed away,
Alas, she did not live to see,
Her daughter, our Queen's Jubilee,
A long life over many years,
Of laughter, joy, and love, and tears,
Her radiant smile, her sense of fun,
She captured the hearts of everyone,
Her Royal duties done with care,
People loved her everywhere,
Her love of gardens - horses too,
Her favourite colour was Royal blue
Her sense of humour, wit and grace,
All are shown in her beautiful face,
Our praises to you will never cease,
Dear Queen Mother
Rest In Peace.

Elizabeth Woodham

A MOTHER'S LOVE

Now I am gone and you're still here,
Think of me with *joy,* my dear.
All my guidance is memory, now,
Use it well, as you know how.
My love for you is paramount,
Support for you was always stout.
When you were low, then I was sad
And at your joy, then I was glad.

Believe in your own self, my love,
All hardships, you can rise above,
Trust in yourself and you'll be fine;
Enjoy your life and take your time
To see, to feel what you know is best:
Living and loving - enjoy them with zest.
Though I'm gone and you're still here,
I'll be nearby, so have no fear.

When times are dark, just think of me,
I'll be close by and hear your plea,
Comfort, I'll try and send to you,
With hope and love, eternally true.

God bless, my love, as always,
                              Mum, xxx.

Maureen Morton

MY GRANDAUGHTER

Olivia Lauren, you're gorgeous
Olivia Lauren, you're great.
You've just turned your smile upon me
And that has sealed my fate.

I'll do anything you desire
Because I am yours to command.
I am willing to jump to attention
And do whatever you demand.

You're such a contented baby
Your smile's like turning on the sun.
You just have to lie there and chuckle
And everyone's hearts you have won.

I think you're a wonderful baby
That is your grandmother's proud boast.
I think that of everyone in the whole world
I'm sure that I love you the most.

Jennie Rippon

A MOTHER'S LOVE

This little poem is written in the hope that you will see
That you really are without a doubt the best mum there could be
I could write a list of reasons but I wouldn't know where to start
Instead I'll take them all and link them directly to your heart
For it's there you hold a love that's immeasurable and true
A strong and steadfast love that flows endlessly from you
This love has been a friend to me in good times and in bad
It has wiped away my tears whenever I was feeling sad
It has listened without judgement to my heartfelt woes and fears
It has advised and encouraged me without fail throughout the years
It has told me how special I am and has seen the things in me
That only those who truly care look hard enough to see
It has taught me what's important in life - the difference between
                                                    right and wrong
It has let me know how it really feels to be loved and to belong
And like the air I breathe, I've grown to need it every day
Knowing that it's there for me means more than words can say
Through these short and simple lines I want to let you see
The difference your love has made to my world and, indeed, to me
So if I could give you just one gift to say thanks for all you do
I'd take all the love you've ever given and give it back to you
With it there'd be peace of mind and a heart that would know no pain
Happiness in abundance so you'd never cry again
And with this gift there'd be good health, and as a final touch
I'd seal it with a note that says 'I love you very much.'

Catriona Toland

MY MUM

Mother is another name for beauty,
She cares for all in pain,
'Rosemarie Healy',
Is my mother's
Name.
Mum I love
You,
Mum, I care,
Mum now for you
I'll always be there,
'Rosemarie Healy',
I love you
From
'Marion Healy',
My mum,
I will be there,
Always,
Mum.

Marion Healy

CHARLOTTE

My one good try to find true love,
O'er 20 years ago,
Just took to wing, like Noah's dove
And settled down below.

My neighbour, George, has model trains,
Which sometimes just go wrong.
For Charlotte, these faults are great gains,
She loves to come along.

I buy her sweets and cuddly toys,
Because she's only six;
As live a wire as most tomboys
Whilst Grandad's trains I fix.

Already, Charlotte knows just how
To melt my old, soft heart.
To please the dog, she'll go 'Bow-wow,'
As round the lawn they dart.

There's nothing shy in Charlotte's wiles
To always have her way;
She breezes in, all full of smiles,
All set to tease and play.

If she were mine, I'd be so proud!
To know her is such pleasure.
I shouldn't say so, right out loud,
But she's a little treasure.

We have to take the dog for walks;
She'll perch upon my shoulder.
Our hugs and kisses, sweethearts' talks
Will fade, as she grows older.

But just for now, I can pretend,
And love this little starlet.
I wish this dream would never end,
For me and dear, sweet Charlotte.

G W Richards

UNTIL DEATH

You're the beauty in my life,
My warrior bride,
My love,
My wife,
You're the one I'll adore,
I want you now,
And even more,
Joyce Healy nee Galloway,
Please,
Joyce,
Never stray,
For you are my love and my life,
Now and forever,
Till death,
My wife.

Eamon John Andrew Healy

I LOVE SATURDAYS!

It's the one day, in the week,
With my loved ones, I get to speak!
All week long, the days drag by,
But Saturday, I'm flying high!

It's my day to telephone,
The time when everyone is home.
In Canada, the hours are wrong,
But Saturdays, we are right on song!

Sometimes, we 'net-meet' by computer,
When I even get to 'see' my daughter!
We laugh, chat, bemoan our plights,
And always put the world to rights!

All that distance disappears,
Hearing her voice, instantly cheers,
I hang onto every word,
Tho' it's often what I've already heard!

Years of being so far apart,
Endear her image, deep in my heart.
Once a year, I go to stay,
Meanwhile Saturday, is my favourite day!

I love Saturdays, every one,
And I thank the Lord, for the telephone.
All of my family are dear to me,
But Saturdays are, reserved for Mandy!

E M Eagle

TO MY MUM

We have been together
All of these years
You have shared my happiness
Also my tears

You've given words of comfort
When life seemed dull and grey
You've made me smile again
And taken my cares away

You've entered my bedroom
Every single night
Placed a kiss on my forehead
And tucked me up tight

Thank you for your love
And your understanding way
I will always love you
Far more than words can say

Now I am grown
One day we will part
And I do know, Mum
It will break your heart

But deep down you'll know
That I will still care
And if you ever need me
I will be there.

Violetta J Ferguson

THE PASSING OF THE NATION'S FAVOURITE GRANDMOTHER

(A remembrance of a fantastic life 1900-2002)

As a child she was brought up in the north,
Little realising just how far she would go forth.
As a teenager she nursed casualties of the Great War
Even then a sense of duty came to the fore.

Wooed and won by a prince who was shy,
She vowed her Bertie was the man she'd stand by.
Married her prince and bore two daughters,
Entered Royal life, like a lamb to the slaughter.

Never really wanted to be the number one Royal,
But the abdication threw her plans into turmoil.
Crowned in Westminster Abbey alongside the new King,
She accepted her destiny and grasped the ring.

Then war came again and the bombing began,
She became a great comfort in a war-ravaged land.
When the Palace was bombed, she said with good grace,
'At least now I can look the East End in the face.'

Then the King died and she was so forlorn,
Didn't really want to carry on alone.
Churchill went to her and wove his magic,
Told her things weren't really that tragic.

She came out of mourning and began to be seen,
As a tower of strength to the nation and our Queen.
Everywhere she went she spread warmth and light,
People travelled for miles to see the sight.

Now that she's gone and can't be replaced,
Her lust for life and living we have to retrace.
The nation will mourn her for a long time to come,
Miss her sense of adventure, laughter and fun.

David Muncaster

GRANDAD'S BIRTHDAY
(In loving memory of Edward (Ted) Bazley)

Grandad, it's your birthday
You would be 82
I hope you and Nan are happy
So happy birthday to you

You were so special
And really kind
Also really funny
You never lost your mind

Grandad, you got older
You never lost your hair
Remember the dancing
Dancing with our Claire

Because you were so special
No words could ever say
How we love and miss you
On this and every day.

Natasha (Tash) Bazley

TO MY GODCHILD

Dear child, what shall I wish for you?
That joy be with you all life through
And sorrow never come a'near?
That you a stranger be to fear?
But no! Such things are worldly-wise,
Truth may bring tears into your eyes,
Yet I would have you love the truth
And grow to age through well-spent youth.

Or shall I wish that wealth untold
Be yours as future years unfold?
Not so, for I have often seen
'Tis not great wealth makes life serene;
And so I pray that God will bless
Your life with peace and happiness.
May wisdom guide you through your ways
And love surround you all your days.

H McCaul

MY MUM

I know that lady over there,
With the wrinkled face
And the vacant stare.

Her youth has gone
There is no trace
Deep lines and shadows line her face.

She sits all day in her little chair
I wonder what she's thinking there
Her mind goes back, mine does too
To memories that you can't undo.

She probably thinks between the tears
Of what she did in her earlier years
Perhaps she thinks of that awful time
When I was young and in my prime.

The war had come, I had to go
To do my bit against the foe.
She drew me close and held me tight,
And said, 'Dear Son, you'll be alright.'

She ran her fingers through my hair
And muttered 'God'll go with you everywhere.'

She startles now when I say 'Hello,'
Disturbed no doubt, but her eyes aglow
Her hand she offers to make the touch
It trembles now, so much, so much.

We talk, but there's not much to say
She's not seen anyone all day
She's glad to see me, that I know
But she won't remember when I go.

Norman S Howells

GRANDCHILDREN

Jodie, Alexander, Rebecca and James
Four very special names
I love them all
Jodie and Alexander are small
Rebecca and James are tall
Into my life they came
Life was never quite the same
They gave me heart when I was low
As the years come and go
Will bring me happiness as they grow.
Jodie, Alexander, Rebecca and James,
Four very special names.

Beryl Turvey

CALLUM AND AMY

My daughter longed to be a grandma
For a very long time.
At last, oh what a joy,
A baby girl and a baby boy.

It's a few months since I saw Callum,
They live so far away,
Photos and progress reports,
Really make my day.

Little Amy lives much nearer,
I see her quite a lot,
She laughs and smiles all day long,
But won't sleep in her cot.

She was one year old last Sunday,
We went to a garden fete,
What a wonderful time we had,
Arrived home rather late.

I think the world of all my children
Just one thing worries me,
On my last birthday,
I was 83.

Kathleen Wheeler

SMUDGE

I fed you every morning
I fed you every night
But now your dish just isn't there
It really isn't right.

Your miaowing sometimes drove me mad
Now the silence does it too
I can't believe that you have gone
I really did love you.

You may have only been a cat
But to me you were my friend
The house seems rather empty
My heart may never mend.

But life goes on as we all know
We had 18 years together
Now rest in peace and you will know
I'll remember you forever.

Evelyn M Cowley

A TOAST TO ELIZABETH II

For 50 long years she has defended the realm,
And a more patriotic Monarch never stood at the helm.
As Queen of the Commonwealth - for Freedom she stands,
And is loved and respected throughout all these lands.
Her devotion to duty has now been as such,
That everyone admires her, and reveres her so much;
Constantly toiling for the good of the state,
So unselfishly giving, caring not of the wait.
Whether a charitable occasion or knighthood bestowed,
Or the opening of Parliament, or a banquet so owed;
All these events and much more does she do,
As our country's Ambassador for the red, white and blue.
From palace to palace throughout the whole world,
Her integrity shines, though some misgivings are hurled.
But *we* are her subjects, the *ones* who do matter,
Which is why we respect her and disregard the latter;
So get out the bunting and drink to 'yours truly',
Thus letting her know that we're not all unruly;
For most of us cherish her, and I sincerely mean . . .
Which is why that 'forever' I want her to stay Queen!
So pick up your glass, and drink to her health,
And say, 'God bless you Ma'am! And the Commonwealth!'
For poorer, as a nation without her we'd be,
Which is why we should celebrate - her Jubilee!

B Colebourn

A ROYAL TRIBUTE

This year is Jubilee year,
50 years upon the throne,
Our Queen so serene and her duty to serve the
Nation and her dedication has surely been shown,
No better Queen we have known,
So true to her duties and the throne.

L Kelley

THE GOLDEN JUBILEE 1952-2002

50 Golden years she's lead
The nation through her reign.
A steadfast life of duty borne
From which the Queen has never waned.

She vowed a vow the day she knew
She was Queen of all the lands
To serve her people with great heart
From far to close at hand.

Her stamina and constant work
Make us all feel proud
Of our nation which has led the world
And we shout her praise aloud.

Changing times she's seen us through
Never wavering from her task.
From great to small - she's done her bit -
And more than we could ask.

The beacon lit this Jubilee
Is a symbol of her life.
To lead and serve with constancy
Through peace and sometimes strife.

Great fortitude through good and bad
Has surely shown her will
To honour her vow and keep her pledge
To lead her people still.

Joys and sorrows touch us all
Many changes have we seen.
With one voice we all will shout
'God bless and save the Queen!'

Mollie D Earl

MICHAEL JACKSON

Michael Jackson
Showman of the Age
Michael Jackson
Is a celebrated name
On the stage.

A singer
A minstrel one may
Have called him yesterday
A star, a celebrity
Of the Age

The thriller
Dance the Dancers
Jackson doing
The famous Moonwalk on the stage

Grammy awards
Fame. Fortune
Everyone shall
Remember his name.

Dizzy Disney tale
Disney Magic
What a fab place
Is Neverland
Fantasy can be really real

Michael Jackson
Will be celebrated
In the Hall of fabulous fame
Reality can be a grim fairy tale.

T Lawrence

NEIGHBOURS

I can't get out to shop myself
But get lots of favours
From loving people where I live
I mean of course my neighbours.
First there's Jim and Mavis,
They are a loving pair?
Mavis never alters
But Jim has lost his hair.
Then there's John and Isa,
One short, the other tall.
Isa loves her knitting
And Johnnie knows it all.
Next to me is dear old Flo
Now she lives all alone,
It's a pity that she suffers
But you never hear her moan.
Mona lives above me
Once, lived upon a farm,
I have known her for many years
Would do nobody harm.
Then there's dear old May
Now she is 92.
She is so active,
You'd think she was 32.
My good friends Jean and Morris
Who have a lovely dog,
Always take it for a walk
But you never see them jog.
Another friend called Peggy
For years we have been friends.
Grew up as teenagers
So I hope it never ends.

Neighbours I have many
So I cannot complain
They help to break monotony
And help to ease the pain.
So to all my neighbours
I would like to say
Stay with us forever
And never move away.

L Newcombe

MOTHER

This poem is written just for you
In thanks and praise for all you do

Not a day goes by when I do not think of how
In those days gone by the treasure chest was full
Dresses, shoes, a whole lot of things you know

Your company was my education
No one ever did the things like you
My life one happy vacation

I grew up thinking I'll always win
Just like you and with a pin

The future always bright and shiny
No fears, no cares just lots of time
Adds up to one life sublime

Your attitude gave the days a glow
Always something new in tow

What a mother, how lucky I am
Never ever stuck in a jam

Money no problem there is a way
We will find how to live today

Lottery, horses, we will have a go
Nothing ventured nothing gained you know

The old chair is empty now
My mother has gone from me

In my heart lives all the memories
Come back Mother dear by my earthly guide
Joined and united with the love that lives inside

How blessed we are to be together
Like old times used to be
No need to worry now, because it's just you and me.

Grace Hicks

BABY

A joyous bundle has at last arrived
To mark the efforts Richard and Sarah contrived
A whole new chapter about to be written
The result of being well and truly smitten

A journey together, in triplicate, ahead
Not one to spoil with feelings of dread
So travel in hope with love and affection
Always giving each other maximum protection

May your voyage of discovery be free and clear
Of serious dangers, problems and worrisome fear
Let your hopes and wishes be totally fulfilled
And life's rewards and prizes keep you thrilled

Good luck Rachael Elizabeth!

A Jessop

JUBILEE POEM

50 years of glorious reign,
Filled with love, joy, sadness and pain.
50 years on the Royal throne,
Our love for our Queen has grown and grown.
50 years of family life,
Not without trouble, toil and strife.
50 years as head of the state,
For the Jubilee, we could hardly wait.
50 years of duties with care,
The people love you - everywhere.
50 years, how the time has flown,
With Commonwealth tours away from home.
50 years - we want you to stay,
For your future - we all will pray.
50 years - thank you - our Queen,
The best 50 years there ever have been!

Elizabeth Woodham

TIME

Time is just a snapshot
Laughing and having fun
Spending time together
Playing in the summer sun.

Time is but a moment
That blankets a dream
Our precious time together
Was seconds it now seems.

Time is a great place
Where hope becomes real
But now that you're resting
You're finally at peace I feel.

Time is just a memory
That God blesses one
If only you were here with me
I love you my wonderful son.

Laura Linfield-Brown

A MOTHER'S LOVE

I hope I brought my mother as much joy as you bring me,
Sometimes you remind me of myself, of how I used to be.
You're only in your teens and still have far to go,
I hope you realise, that I love you so.

Remember that I'm always here,
To share your laughter and your fears.
Whatever you do, or choose to be,
You'll always have love from me.

From the minute you were born and dressed in lace,
You had the sun shining from your face.
To date in life, you've done your best,
Each day you fill, full of zest.

Things you've said and things you've done
It's a pleasure, being your mum.

Ann Jones

MY PARENTS

They've always been there for me, you see
But when they are gone how will I be?
I dread to think of that time to come
But come it will, and it won't be undone.

I was born in London during the war
I'm three score years, and then some more!
I've had an age to appreciate them longer
I'm sure it's made the family stuff stronger.

We don't kiss and cuddle, we're not that sort
But then, do you think I ought
To tell them I love them every day
But it's not the type of thing I say.

I try to be there to ease their pain
To oil the wheels of life's fast train.
They can't keep pace with life's frantic tear
When no one has time to stand and stare.

They've always been there for laugh and a chat
And in the past bore the brunt of my flack.
But now I cherish the things they say
To remember forever and a day.

They're parents and friends on whom I depended
Cos their offers of help were open-ended.
'Top brick off the chimney' Dad always says
When asking for favours in bygone days.

Their advice and wisdom were always heeded
In years gone by when it was needed.
But now I try to be their rod of iron
To be always there for them to rely on.

The void will be awful when I have them no more
It will go deep to my very core!

Joan Edwards

AMANDA

My little grandaughter
was born today.
She was six weeks early.
She just didn't want to wait.
I felt so proud to see her born
a day I won't forget.
I promise to be there
in love or in pain.
My grandaughter is special
I'll be there every day.

Amanda Houghton

BEST FRIEND

With the stress and strain of daily life
It's sometimes hard to cope
But from the moment I was born
My best friend gave me hope.

She loves me unconditionally,
She's there to dry my tears
And she has seen my life evolve
Unfolding through the years.

My friend is always there for me,
She always understands.
She give me strength to carry on
And never makes demands.

My judge and jury she is not
'Though I'm not always right.
I wonder at her wisdom:
She seems to know what's right.

I may not always find the words
To say how much I care.
I'm filled with silent gratitude
For this bond that we share.

I love her very, very much.
A happy tune I hum.
The song is 'Mother's Melody'.
My best friend is my mum.

Melanie Swan-Liddell

MY MOTHER MY DEAR

I look up at the stars in the clear night sky,
Are you on one of them now as it's passing by.
Are you on a cloud that floats by on the breeze,
Or up in the branches of the tallest oak tree.
I think of the day when you left me behind,
And things that you taught me fill my mind.
There was no end to your love, no end to your care,
Then one day I looked up and your were not there.
The things you'd done, the things you'd said,
Come rushing and swirling through my head.
I can picture, your smiling face and silver hair so clear,
In my heart you're still with me my mother, my dear.

S M Wilkinson

MOTHER

You are gentle, sweet and kind
Another like you would be hard to find.
To us children you are strong
Teaching us right from wrong.
Showing each of us things to do
Imparting to us your point of view.
Giving a love that's really meant
Hoping we grow up strong and decent
And live our lives right to the end
Loving each other as relation and friend.
Words of wisdom on how to live
Words that only a mother can give.
Give to us children when we part
Give to us children from your heart.

Diana Daley

To My Father, P T W Hatton

Third of four sons, my father was,
    One sister led the line,
Born of good sturdy Midlands' stock
    Where Saxon and Dane combine.
Fair-haired, blue-eyed and ruddy-cheeked,
    He and his brother Jack
Were models of the Saxon kin
    From generations back.
You'd say, no Norman conqueror had ever thinned their blood;
From 'Settlement below the hill' with Harold they might have stood.

An English pride, an English strength,
    Complete integrity,
My father taught without a word;
    Few like him one can see.
Like Jacob, seven years he served
    Before he could be wed.
'The only unselfish man I've known,'
    So his wife's sister said.
Music he wrote, and merry verse,
    Gardened both flowers and fruit,
Used tools in advance of DIY.
    His loved wife's plans to suit.
But no grandchilden came his way -
    It seems a wicked waste -
The long line ends - no lesser man
    Could suit his daughter's taste.
No civic honours crowned his name, but many a faithful friend
Respected, loved and mourned for him, 'Mere English' to the end.

Kathleen M Hatton

A TRILOGY OF YESTERYEAR
(This poem is dedicated in loving memory of my mother)

A Tragic Fairy Tale - 1800's
Mother's great aunt worked in a Paisley jute mill at the reel,
The owner's son remarked her beauty and demeanour genteel.
Duly wed combining honeymoon and business, cruising for a year
Returning to Broomielaw Docks, the fairy tale was doomed I fear.
Great Aunt died giving birth to twin boys, they were fine
Alas life can with cruel fate her blessings entwine.

Too Happy - Early 1900's
Grandma did not care for her daughter's letters home
Went, found her treated more as a slave and a drone
From a minister's family, whisked her away, goodbye to that lot!
Aunt then married a blacksmith, yet told her sister, too happy
                                                        she thought.
When pregnant an old Spey wife kept her at the door one day
Premonition perhaps she'd had, for Nemesis came its way
Aunt developed pneumonia, she and unborn baby died
Family and sister just sighed and cried and cried.

A Tragic Romance - Early 1900's
Mother's eldest sister once met a young man
At an aunt's London guest house the romance began
He visited Glasgow as auld a reekie as Edinburgh then known.
Met the family but sadly emigrated to Canada alone.
Returning, hoping Aunt would leave her mother, have a change of mind
A passenger aboard ill-fated Lusitania, sunk, his body they never
                                                        did find.
The song 'Bow Bells' for the lovers would be an apt them
As a lovely lady lost her man and life's sweet magic dream.

Christina Craig Harkness

POLLY'S GRADUATION

February the 13th,
Two thousand and two,
a day to remember
for your family and you.

It is all the hard work
and passes achieved,
plus the willing support
you so nobly received.

Much prayer here has reached Him,
God knew you were keen,
with the deepest desire
and much faith He has seen.

A day of true blessing
our God has been true,
a day of Graduation
has been chosen for you.

Mary Smith

MOTHER'S PRIDE

Little curls of wispy hair
a button nose and skin so fair.
Two little eyes of dreamy blue
it's wonderful to look at you.

One of nature's marvellous gifts
to be nurtured, loved and treasured.
Nothing can compare to you
your value can't be measured.

You are absolutely perfect
from your head down to your toes.
Every time I look at you
my love just grows and grows.

Sometimes I feel my heart will burst with pride
for I've been blessed
with the wonder that is little you
you've brought such happiness.

I'll love you till I'm old and grey
and some day you will see
what having a son as perfect as you
has really meant to me.

Grace McGregor

AUNTIE FLO

Dear Auntie Flo words cannot say
How much I miss you everyday,
For half my lifetime you are there
So wise, supportive, always fair,
Of earthly treasures you had few
But did whatever you could do
And what you did was without price
Your wisdom, love and good advice
There were so many laughs we shared
For pride and swank you never cared
I miss you say 'How's life with you?'
You made my troubles seem so few.
I can't believe at ninety three
So young at heart you were to me.
I miss our 'natters' on the phone
The sense of being not alone
We shared those memories of yore
Hard times and good and so much more
Our childhood games, the wartime stress,
The rationed food and 30's dress,
Our teenage years and teenage tears
The problems of old age and fears.
Dear Flo you cheered the saddest day
And now an OAP I say
Of all the gold and wealth on earth
You were far, far above their worth
I prayed you'd have that peaceful end
But oh dear Flo - I miss my friend.

S A Baker

UNCLE LEN

This is the shed where he sheltered from the showers,
On this allotment where he spent his hours.
Digging double digging, doubled up with pain,
'Got to finish this bit afore it comes on to rain.'

And hung on a nail his old tweed jacket,
In the pocket some string and an old seed packet.
And see, now faded, the photo he carried,
In yesterday's sunshine, the girl he never married.

He began this allotment just after the war,
And from this Middlesex clay fed a family of four.
In spite of the rain and in spite of the drought,
He worked it and weeded it week in and week out.

At horticultural shows he 'walked off' with the prizes,
For his leeks and his onions of prize winning sizes.
Then off to the pub at the end of his labours,
For a laugh and a pint with his friends and his neighbours.

On this gloomy day in winter, inside this creaking shed,
Memories of days gone by go round inside my head.
As I look up I seem to see the gardener's spirit rise,
Borne away on a wisp of smoke to vanish in the skies.

No more the squelch of his booted feet,
Will trudge the soft clay between rows of beet.
Now uncut cabbages stand rotting in the rain,
Of last season's runner beans, only the sticks remain.

His tools are left idle, the plot grows over,
Nature will triumph with her grass and her clover.
The gardener's gone home, gone to his rest.
The harvester of harvesters only picks the best.

Ron Lamerton

THE GUARDIAN SPIRIT

With human eyes you cannot see,
The spirit that you knew as me,
But I am never far away,
And I am with you all the way.

I'm with you through the good and bad,
I'm with you when your heart is glad,
Through times of pain, despair and sorrow,
And all the heartaches of tomorrow.

My never changing love for you
Is still as deep, as warm, as true;
No force can break the bond we share,
Though I am here, and you are there.

David Webb

QUEEN ELIZABETH, OUR QUEEN MOTHER

On 30th March 2002
our sovereign's mother died;
The next ten days the nation mourned
and many people cried.
With her magical smile and gentle touch
one never felt alone;
She was a mother to the nation
as well as to the throne.

During war time in this country
our Queen and King stood proud;
They toured the bomb hit cities
and mingled with the crowd.
King and Queen went side by side
throughout those war-torn years;
They did not run nor hide away
they shared the nation's tears.

Then all too soon her 'Bertie' died
a sad and tragic day;
His Queen left broken-hearted
in her mourning went away.
With her role as Queen now over
a new one came to light;
That of the dear Queen Mother
which she honoured with all her might.

She warmed the hearts of many
to whom she gave so much;
She was Regal and majestic
yet had the 'common' touch.
Her warm and caring nature
is one we'll not forget;
She touched the hearts of everyone
no matter whom she met.

Although Regal and majestic
as she saw her duties through;
This lady had a sense of fun
and could let her hair down too.
She shared a joke with many
loved her sport and a tipple or two;
She was full of love and laughter
which throughout her life shone through.

God bless you Queen Elizabeth
as you now lay at rest;
Besides your darling 'Bertie'
the one you loved the best.
It is an ending of one era
and the beginning of another.
You'll be in our hearts forever more
Queen Elizabeth, our Queen Mother.

Ann Forshaw

MY FATHER

With hat in hand and smiling face
He kissed me with his careless grace;
And then walked out beyond the door.
Goodbye, it was, forevermore.
Back he went, across the sea.
Did he ever think of me?

A rush of tears invades my eyes
For he's now gone, beyond replies;
And I have come to this fair place
The country of my father's race
And found in every vale and rise;
A beauty kin to Paradise.

Gwyneth Bacon

QUEEN MOTHER

On the 9th of April, in 2002
Everybody filled with grief, for someone who
Was known to all as the Queen Mother
Both popular and genuine like no other.

Her daughter, grandchildren, and many more too
Showed their respect with the farewell 'do'
People and service folk from every rank
Lined the streets for the 'cortège' to flank.

Some folk had queued for hours on end
To say goodbye to their loyal friend
A grand old lady of 101
Who started her life, before most had begun.

The sun shone down on one and all
As the 'remains' were removed from Westminster Hall
To the Cathedral for a Service, and journey on
To Windsor to lie, in the plot by her husband, long gone.

The family now feeling that awful strain
Of the loss of a loved one, while hiding their pain
From the TV camera with pictures to see
Keeping us all informed of what was to be.

Now the Funeral has ended, as we all know
And hope it will be a while for the country to go
To see another pageant in full array
Like that sunny April morning, a sad sombre day.

Imelda Fitzsimons

OUR QUEEN MUM

She was everyone's Mum
Our Queen Mum
She'd give you a wave
A memory you'd save
She'd love the flowers
It was worth standing hours
She was the best nan
A magical gran
Nothing she'd do by half
Such humour she'd make everybody laugh
She was such a special one
No one believed she was 101
Her years of work and devotion
Left us with such emotion
We now have to say goodnight
To someone so special and so right.

Linda Stevens

REMEMBERED FOREVER

At Westminster your coffin stands alone,
Mourners' wait in silence, your soul has flown,
Up into the stars and the heavens above,
Is the soul of the Queen Mother filled with love.

Elizabeth and George are united again,
Under the stars lit by God's flame,
We can all shed tears that she's gone,
But also smile because she lived long.

Mourner's wait in silence and remember,
Our beloved Queen's Mum, she's so tender,
In the great wars united we won,
Our Queen Mother was so full of fun.

Now she's united with George, she can dance,
In the ghostly halls of Buckingham Palace,
And in Windsor dancing under God's stars,
Where Royal ghosts dance and drive fast cars.

But saying all this one thing is true,
We will remember forever your love shining through
Queen Mum, God bless and thanks,
With a little tot of gin and all your pranks . . .

Edward Healy

UNCLE BOB

He was not really 'Uncle' Bob at all,
But being a close friend of the family,
Our children three were always pleased to call
Him 'Uncle', which he accepted happily.

I met him first on staff at school where we
Both taught French. He'd been scholar at Stowe
In its early days, then Corpus Christi,
With the European 'Grand Tour' to follow.

Gunner captain in the war, in Norway,
Scotland, Europe, where in Intelligence
O'er aerial photo until he held sway.
Stories we'd swap of wartime experience!

He left the school to care for ailing mother
In lovely Sussex home, the Downs before.
He'd younger sibling twins, sister, brother,
Who gave his life for Country in the War.

In holidays he'd have us down to stay.
He'd drive us through the Sussex countryside
To view old houses, castles on the way . . .
Was always such a knowledgeable guide.

Godfather to our youngest child, he showed
A helpful interest in the education
Of all three, whom, in their teens, he took by road
On tour of Austria in their vacation.

He travelled much. He'd stay a day or two
To brief school Travel Club on latest trip
And show his films, intriguing background to
His traveller's tales by plane, car, train and ship.

Seat on County Council he didn't enjoy;
Party politics drove him to distraction.
School governor, magistrate were more his ploy,
Education and justice the attraction.

We grieved his distant, sad, untimely end.
We miss him still but time can never rob
Us of fond memories of a trusted friend,
Our caring, wise and generous Uncle Bob.

Geoffrey Matthews

GRANDAUGHTER

Come grandaughter kneel with me,
Close your eyes so you can't see,
Press your palms close together,
Remember this prayer for ever and ever.
For the Lord's prayer we will say,
On this very special day,
Repeat these words I say to you
And God will help you stay brand new.
Likechildren we must go to Him,
So as we pray just we two
For to this church come but a few,
God's presence is all about,
That dear child there is no doubt.

Ann Iverson

BOBBIE

Dearest Bobbie has gone away,
Sadly he there will stay.
He went to sleep without a fuss.
Just put down his head knowing he must.

He had been so ill for many a day,
But wouldn't give in and wagged his tail,
He loved us all, and showed it well,
Protecting us from strangers and
Dangers which might prevail.

From the very start, he was beloved
I enjoyed his company, his play was like honey,
He pranced and rolled about in fun,
When he was happy and had a full tum.

His eyes told of his love for me,
His joyfulness was there to see,
Entwined in fun we lived in a bubble,
Our life was a cameo of beauty doubled.

I shall miss him every hour of every day,
But he's at peace and in no pain,
I hope he's playing and having fun,
On a green lawn, rolling in the sun.

Betsy Williams

My Dad

My dad he was a naval man in two world wars served he
for 28 years the Seven Seas he did sail,
a proud man who served in ships of grey in the Royal Navy
and the medals on his chest are proof his loyalty did not fail.
When serving in the Arctic Seas they told him his son is born
another two years to pass before homeward he could be,
a love for me and his duty to the crown he would be torn
until the day to his family and his son to hold and see.

Around the world he sailed evermore
writing letters to Mum and me,
is this a sailor's duty chore
when will my dad come home for us to see?
When the time came for him to sail no more
so glad were my mum to know he was homeward bound,
then came that conflict the second world war
from mum's bedroom I heard a sobbing sound.
I never had the joy of having a dad
at home each night and weekend,
a life without a father can be sad
but proud of him I am, my dad, our country to defend.

John Clarke

GRANDPA

Grandpa used to keep a store of lotions and pill
so if a neighbour had animals hurt or ill,
Grandpa could cure them, if within his power
and made himself available at any hour.
In outlying villages, few vets were found,
neighbours trusted Grandpa, knew his knowledge was sound.
He was well thought of in the community,
a son of the Dorset soil . . . Grandpa to me.

Valerie Ovais

PASSING OF A QUEEN CONSORT

Our lovely Queen Mother has gone to her rest.
What a beautiful lady, and so full of zest.
So gracious, charming, witty and kind.
These are the memories, which she left behind.

A help to her husband, when the going was tough
She encouraged him greatly through smooth times and rough.
The public adored her in war and in peace.
She prayed with her people that conflict would cease.

We remember the Queen in her Jubilee Year.
Wishing her loved ones could be with her here.
To join celebration; laughter and fun
Her mum would have loved it at 101.

We look at her pictures all down through the years
Amid all the sorrows, the joys and the tears.
We thank God for her life, and when things seem quite glum
We remember with fondness our lovely Queen Mum.

Maureen Anderson

THANKS

Thanks for listening when I'm down,
Thanks for always being around,
You say you'll be there - then you're not!
Your excuse is - you forgot!
I need you sometimes when you're not there -
But I know you'll always care!
What am I going to do when you're gone -
How am I ever going to get along?
Then who am I going to share my
High and lows as along life's road we go?
I'd like to think you'll always be there -
But I know life isn't always fair!
I'd like to say - while I can -
Thanks for listening
Through my highs and lows
As along life's road we go!
Thanks.

Norma Spillett

FOR MUM, A POEM

You bore me into this life,
  Tended me, then, with
Your flowing n'golden hair. So proud
  Of you, my kith;
And not so loud
  In the days, when at your knee . . .

Then you spoke, calling me Rich!
  So poor am I; but, your cheer
Brought my love to a pitch,
  N'then you gave me . . .(your) fear
But, one day - outa the ditch,
  We shall be united: So, dear!

There, again, at the gardens
  We brought our lines t'completion;
N'nothing' you say, hardens
  The way of the world's deletion . . .
For all of us (full) o'the pardons
  That allow our indiscretion.

N'where are you now?
  Like, I wanna believe in your good;
And the prow, n' the Plough
  Of the fellowship, and the seed
Demand that, somehow: Your need
  Be met, with the care (you) gave me?

Take your time t'be still -
  Like those honoured moments, of family
When you thought me 'ill'
  And, once or twice, got next t'me
When I turned it all to the quill
  And ended, with, praising thee!

Anon

BELINDA BLUE EYES
(Dedicated to Lesley)

A small box was found by me, draped
in cobwebs, dust and grime.
Blowing all these things away they had been
there for a long, long time.
I wondered what the box would display
so I opened it with care
and just in case something fragile was
perhaps concealed in there.
A scruffy something peered up at me
one-eyed bedraggled and worn
that my face lit up of my treasured find
of a doll so dirty, and faded, with time.
But one so beautiful when bought new
Belinda Blue Eyes, is it really you.

Pauline Potts

FAREWELL

Pomp and pageantry, all regiments seen
With Air Force and Navy, lined streets for a Queen,
An elderly lady gone to rest
By all accounts, one of the best.
A favourite Royal who lived a long life
Witnessing troubles, wars and strife.
A widow of many years we record,
Her presence requested, no time to be bored.
Supporting the Monarchy to her meant all,
In the 30's she thought it would fall.
Now she has gone, we witness the scene
In the Abbey of Royalty, the most there has been
For forty odd years, since her husband the King
Now she will join him at Windsor this spring.
Sadness and tears from the family so dear,
Prying cameras reported each tear.
In sunshine and sorrow we said our farewell
To a grand old lady, the Queen Mother, we tell
Of her staff and friends of lowly birth
Who shared with her many tales, and mirth.
They too at the Abbey paid their respect
To this Queen who ruled, they will never forget.
We turn a page in our history now,
Our present Queen will show us how,
To modernise the ancient ways
Improving the Monarchy for future days . . .
Our hard working Queen we wish her well
The support of her people and time, will tell.

P Evans

QUEEN MOTHER

A time to live and a time to die
Even for the lady in the public eye.
We all will miss her now she has passed away
But in our hearts she will always stay.
She was born to be our beloved Queen,
One of the best our Nation has seen.
A pillar of strength to all whom she knew,
A figure of courage, simply one of the few.
Her life was blessed with long happy years.
It was lived to the full with all she held dear.
She was proud of her country, her people as well,
Her devotion to duty was not hard to tell.
During the war years, a comfort to all,
Ever ready and waiting to answer a call.
Her presence brought hope to those who were sad,
It lightened their load, it made them feel glad.
And now it is time that we must carry on
As best as we can since she has now gone.
We'll remember with joy, we'll remember with pride,
The wonderful lady who once stood by our side.

Margaret Garvie

MY WIFE

My wife is the best, you cannot dispute
and others they think, she's really quite cute.
She's always around when times get too tough
and I never know how to thank her enough.

One I can talk to when things seem so bad
and she gives me comfort when I'm feeling sad.
I know we'll be together right up to the end,
because my dear wife is also my friend.

Steve Elson

GABBY

Gorgeous Gabby, we will never forget,
was the sweetest little pet.
We lost her in 1999,
obviously it was her time.

She gave us lots of pleasure,
was certainly a little treasure.
Four boys and a girl in the litter,
being the only female, we did pick her.

We nicknamed her Custard Pie Face,
and with her mum Cleo, she did race.
She miaowed a heck of a lot,
and attention she always got.

Never short of a purr,
had grey, orange and white fur.
She was a most affectionate cat,
often we did her back pat.

Birds were her favourite snack,
now she's gone we have them back.
Fear Gabby did have not,
up to mischief she always got.

A scruffy little fur ball,
often found lying on her wall.
Her presence we sadly miss,
we send you Gabbs, *a big kiss.*

Kateryna Mazelan (nee Kozak)

MUM

I'm sure when you were young
You must have had demands,
To sail seas, watch sunsets,
All in foreign lands.
You probably had some fun,
Throughout your teenage years,
I bet you had great friends
With whom you shared your laughter and your tears.
And of course you fell in love
With a very special man,
Although you were still young
Your life together you could plan.
Your first child was a boy,
A girl, your second one.
I bet it made you wonder,
Where has my own life gone?
Grazed knees, tears, runny noses,
Smiles, laughter and love.
Praise, encouragement, patience, hugs,
Were you sent from up above?
You've listened to our problems,
You let us lean on you,
Given everything we've asked for,
And things we haven't too.
Now we're both much older.
Our own mistakes we've made,
With patience and understanding,
Your love is still displayed.
We don't show you that we love you
Or thank you for being there,
Always taking it for granted,
The way you show you care.

Whenever you feel lonely,
Or if you're sad and low,
Wondering what you've done with life
Or what you've got to show.
Take a look at us together,
All the things you've done for us,
Sacrifices that you've made,
We know that it's because,
You're a very special person,
Special qualities you have as well,
This poem's to show our love,
Although in words we cannot tell,
How very much you mean to us,
Like you, we hope we'll be,
You've given us unconditional love,
Always us, not I or me,
So to you we're both so grateful,
That fate made you our mum.
We thank you for our lives
And the future that is to come.
If the fate that brought us together,
Should part us from one another,
We'll remember, we were lucky,
To have a devoted, loving mother.

Nicola J Horridge

THANK YOU FOR BEING YOU

(Dedicated to the memory of my good friend
Mick Carpenter, who died May 2002)

Thank you for being you
For always being there.
Helping me in my moments of deep despair.
Thank you for being you.

It was to you that I turned to
When my world fell apart
With your love and understanding
You gave me strength to make a new start.

Thank you for being my friend
For helping me sort out what to do
For giving me courage and hope to carry on
Thank you for being you.

K Arblaster

MY DAUGHTER, GOLDEN LYNN

My daughter Lynn is beautiful
Of that there is no doubt
God's given me a daughter
I'd like to tell the world about.

'All that glitters is not gold'
That's how the saying goes
But my Lynn is flawless
From the top of her head
To the tips of her toes.

Lynn has turned 50,
A grandmother of four
But you would hardly believe it
If she came knocking on your door.

I call her Golden Lynn
The apple of my eye
She also has an inner beauty
For sure I tell you no lie.

Stay as sweet as you are my lovely Lynn
You make my old heart glad
You're the golden girl of all time
Love you, your dear old dad.

JP
Dad xx

MY POEM FOR JED

(Aged 8)

Lying fast asleep in bed
I crept in to look at Jed
Angel face and hair so fair
Full of grace, just lying there.

Little chest moved up and down
First a smile and then a frown
Wondered just what was he dreaming
Running, laughing, playing, scheming?

Just a little boy asleep
Then I took another peep
A little hero I could see
An angel who'd been sent to me.

I dropped to my knees in prayer
Ran my fingers through his hair
He has filled my life with joy
Thank you Lord for this sweet boy.

Hazel Phillips

UNTITLED

I have a little tabby cat, Cleo is her name
Since she came along and adopted me
My life is not the same.
Under the table she has placed four feet
And now dictates what she will eat.
When I try once again, the balance to turn
Her looks say 'Will you never learn?
I rule the roost in this house!
And when you are good I bring you a mouse.'
I'm sure that she loves me just the same
Tho' I know I'm just a pawn in her little game.
By and large, we live side by side
She has become my little Jekyll and Hyde
I love her despite all her odd turns
A good home and me seems all that she yearns.

M Brazier

A Song For Liam

Why did you go?
Why didn't you stay?
I know something happened in your life,
But I'm not allowed to say.
I can't express how much you mean to me,
So please let me know why you left me that way.

So Liam,
This song is for you.
I hope someone, somewhere is loving you.
Now you have gone,
I need to say,
How much I love you.

So Liam,
I keep remembering,
All the good times we had,
Now those days are dead and buried,
And in the past,
But I want to look to the future,
And pray that you will come back to me some day.
I hope this isn't a dream,
For both you and me,
So let me finish by saying, 'I love you.'

Lisa Frith - (his sister aged 20 years)

CAROLINE

Caroline you are so fine, Oh little sister of mine,
you make my day seem bright, you make everything alright
you have a smile so sunny, you pull faces that are funny,
you are my little honey, Oh little sister of mine.

You have lovely bright red hair, you are kind and always share,
I love it when you are there, Oh little sister of mine,
you have freckles that look so cute, you really are a beaut'
you love to play the hoot, Oh little sister of mine.

When Dad brings me home, I love to see you there
with my mum and my two brothers, all sat in Dad's favourite chair
we all sit down to tea, you like to sit near me
Mmm! Burgers for our tea. Oh little sister of mine.

Andy Douglas

MY FRIEND

I've got a good friend called Sarah
I've known for just two years.
Whenever I am feeling sad
Her smile dries up my tears.

We've shared good times
And sometimes bad
But knowing we're there for each other
Makes us glad.

We will keep our friendship
And not let each other down
Because when you've a good friend
There is no need to frown.

Jenny Duff

FLYING FREE

Two souls now united and free
Elizabeth and George
He was once our sovereign King
She was the Queen Mum.
At Westminster Abbey your coffin
Stands in silence
Mourners pass, shedding tears
We have said our goodbyes
Now fly, fly away
Up with the angels
She's gone
She smiled
At me
Our Queen Mum
Now she's dead
But she's free.

Joyce Healy

TIONI, MY SISTER

When I think of you I feel excited inside,
I have a lot of feelings that I cannot hide,
I'm glad you're my sister
And when I hold you, I always shake inside.

The first time I saw you, Mum had a scan,
You weren't even born yet, I was already a fan.
I'm glad you're my sister
And when I hold you I always shake inside.

When I first looked at you my heart went to jelly,
Butterflies were flying around in my belly,
I'm glad you're my sister
And when I hold you I always shake inside.

I remember the day my heart skipped a beat,
You came into my life, I had one big treat
I'm glad you're my sister
And when I hold you I always shake inside.

The day that you were born you left me breathless,
That's why I play our song,
I suppose you could guess
I'm glad you're my sister
And when I hold you I always shake inside.

Jonathon Halls

SHE'S SO SPECIAL

I'm writing this especially for you.
In every way, in all you do,
when I needed to be, you set me free,
when I needed to cry you asked me 'Why?'
So I choose this day to say to you,
I love you Mum . . .
through and through.

Charlene Soan

WORTH THE WAIT

We could not wait until, the day that you were born
To have a little grandchild to call our very own.

To hear what people say, they make your life complete
We thought that they were joking, to say the very least.

But every word was true and we can plainly see,
That you were sent from Heaven, for your grandad and me.

Kathleen South

OUR GRANDCHILDREN

Our grandchildren, Jade, Dayle and Rhys
Well-behaved, they give us joy, comfort, love and peace.
Jade, 14, Dayle, 11, Rhys, 8, Oh! They are yearning
To live a life so full, exciting, full of learning
We go to church each Sunday,
We hope from this they will learn love and peace,
To share and care for others in this world, and never cease.
For we, as grandparents, must show a world which cares
Children who grow up happy and what they've got, with others share.
Through all their years they've given us such pleasure and delight
When things go wrong, they give a hug, their love makes life so bright.
We worry what the future for these three will hold
But surrounded with love they will grow up bold.
To face life at which anything can throw
And catch their dreams and watch them grow.
Our love for them will never fade
Whatever they do they will make our grade.
For after all is said and done
Love is free and never won.
So as we watch them day by day
Their loving parents often say
'In spite of all the ups and downs,
Tears and tantrums, smiles and frowns,
It's all worthwhile for the love they bring.'
Fills all their lives and the rafters ring
With happy voices joined together
To face anything, in any weather.

Rita Fletcher

THE QUEEN MUM
(At her passing)

How can we express today, the sorrow in our heart,
Only those alone can say, for they themselves took part.
The evacuation of the children, the embarking of our men,
The despair of the women, when would we see them again?

The destruction of our cities, the burial of our dead
The sleepless nights, the no-news days,
The queuing up for bread.

The Queen was there, 'God bless her heart',
By the King's side, right from the start.
Talking to victims that had been bombed out,
Giving sympathy, hope and encouragement, on her walkabout.

'Our home was bombed too,' she was heard to say,
'Now I feel at one with you, in every way.
We will get through it, if we all play our part.'
Making time to listen, she gladdened every heart.

She was like a ray of sunshine,
Brightening up our day,
With a smile, a laugh, oft times a wave
As she went upon her way.

We remember her best in the darkest of days
While Britain fought hard, the world to save.
She inspired us all, as a mother, wife and Queen.
As a fitting tribute to her passing,
'Let our tears be seen.'

Madge Goodman

JAMIE

I love the way he smiles at me and the twinkle in his eye
I love the hands that reach for me, I love to hear him sigh.
This little love from heaven, this symbol of so much joy
I love to love him always, this golden-haired little boy.

No angel could be brighter, no star to match his fame
None are more endearing, no other of his name
Every moment shared with him, every hour, every minute
All my love I'll give to him, and it will know no limit.

F Cooper

PETE AND JESS

Pete is a storeman,
Pete is my mate,
He wanted to get married,
He just couldn't wait.

Then he met a young girl,
Jessie was her name,
Pete said 'You'll do for me'
Jessie said the same.

So they said 'We'd best get wed,
September 1st, the day.
We'll have a little party
Then we'll go away.'

To a sun-filled land they flew away
Their little hearts on fire
With dreams of rides
And eventides
Filled with their hearts' desires.

Three weeks have passed
They're back at last
Pete's back at work with me.
While Jessie tends the dentist's chair
And dreams of what's to be.

So good luck Pete and Jessie,
May your life be like a song
the song and wish I give to you
Is just 'Stay forever young'.

A year now has gone
They still sing their song
Of love and harmony.
But louder still,
For what a thrill
Once two, they now are three!

Peter West

I SAT ALONE

I sat alone without my dad.
I felt happy for him, but for me, very sad.
I asked myself questions, if, why and how?
I don't know the answers,
At least not for now.
I thought of all the times we'd shared;
How he had taught me, scolded me, cared.
I wondered if he was watching me now;
I couldn't be sure, but I thought so somehow.
I felt him near me, yet so far away;
Will I ever see him again one day?
Or only in photographs, memories, books,
To remind me of how he looked.

I sat alone without my dad.
I felt happy for him, but for me, very sad.
I needed his shoulder to cry on right then
But it wasn't there - just my paper and pen.
I loved you dear Daddy - I'm sure that you knew
And I know in my heart that you loved me too.

Susanne Semmence

MARILYN MONROE

(75 years a celebration)

M arilyn Monroe, a goddess and a woman tour de force,
A mbitions and fantasies she always fulfilled, those of men of course,
R esplendent on screen, a vision to behold and that seduced,
I mage superseded talent - the myth that the Hollywood
                                    machine produced,
L ove for herself and respect she craved, alas with little success,
Y ellow tresses with a body to die for, hid her personal life - a mess.
'N iagara', was awesome, as was 'Some Like It Hot' and she
                    discovered 'How To Marry A Millionaire'
M arriage, long-term proved elusive and unhappiness came with
                                    every affair,
O ver the course of time she became tormented and sad,
N ever did she conquer childhood demons, which made her
                                    bitter and mad,
R etreating into seclusion during periods from forces she perceived
                                    as bad.
O verdosed, she died aged 36, alone and a victim of her creation,
E ternally her legend lives on, let's join in the celebration.

F Buliciri

JOSIE

You're deft at arms length keeping
While holding rapt attention.
You dazzle with your eyes
But conceal your inner intention.
You speak from your heart
But deliberate in your head
Though your streak of independence
Leaves you empty in your bed.
You press your liberated views
Yet crave the social whirl
And grace such company with delight
Like a charming little girl.
You draw fans like a magnate
Yet always leave alone
You say that you will call again
Yet seldom on the phone.
I adore your upbeat vocal tone
From that unexpected call
If you say you're on a high tonight
I will catch you when you fall.
Your stance is non-committal
And I love the things you do
But your garrulous bravado's diaphanous
Because I can see through you.

Michael Gardner

Simple Thanks

In my needing time of pain,
They all deserted me away,
You stood by me, gave me hope
You said you'll be there as a friend.

My friend, you have been more than that,
My hope and strength to carry on.
I won't forget your words of praise,
They linger to me from this day.

Chandra

ODE TO A NEWBORN CHILD

Oh captured innocence, lying there,
So small against the giant world;
With downy skin and wisps of hair
And tiny fingers, tightly curled:
Are you the miracle of life,
The mystery of man's new birth?
And are you fitted for the strife,
The constant struggle here on earth?

And as I gaze upon your form
My heart o'er filled with tender love,
And feel your breath so sweet and warm,
I sense the presence up above
Of something great, an awesome being,
Omnipotent, both old and new,
Whose guiding visage, ever-seeing,
Directs the arms which cradle you.

Oh child of mine, what will you be,
When in this nurturing love you grow?
All woollen-wrapped upon my knee,
Contented mouth like Cupid's bow.
My hopes and dreams, my failures, fears
Are all tight-held within this shawl;
And will the passing of the years
Strip back the truth, revealing all?

Oh tiny child, on such as you
Unspoiled and free from lust and greed,
Rest all man's hopes for life anew,
A second chance, from shackles freed.
So what a tender burden this;
How anxiously I play my part,
While you sleep on, in newborn bliss,
Oh tiny stripling of my heart.

Gwen Cameron

A FEW WORDS
(For Sean, Susan, Karen, Daniel & Luke)

Sometimes it's hard to put into words
Or describe how much I think about you all
For without you
I would be lost, like a pebble tossed to sea
I have been sad but your voices have cheered me
I have been lonely but you have brought so much happiness
For everything you have done, big or small
And for the greatest gift of all, to love and be loved . . . *thanks.*

David Tye

FAREWELL TO MY FRIEND, MARK

Such a dear friend Mark was, he taught me all I know
about computers you know.
A computer tech now that's me, trying to carry on Mark's work
you see, by being all I can be.
A radio ham Mark used to be, helping people like you and me
from any of the danger we were in.

Mark was very clever and very bright, that's how he was
with you and me
Mark was a biker of his kind, with a very wonderful mind.

He used to surf the Interment and have a page that you have to glance.
Then one day he said 'goodbye' to surf the Internet in the sky.
Where angels fly by on a highway that's not seen by you or I.

Where bikers find their paradise in a world with one eye.
The one passageway to that place that is,
heavenly blessed ready for you and I.

Gemma Darling

THE TRAMP

Most people know him as Old Ben
He is a familiar figure about the town,
I should imagine that he must walk miles in a day
Never allowing the weather to get him down.

He has untidy hair and he wears a beard
Although he has a kindly face,
One of his boots is tied up with string
Instead of a proper lace.

You will often see him sitting on a bench in the park
Watching the mothers with their children at play,
He has a thought that they feel sorry for him
Although he would not want his life any other way.

Cheeky schoolboys would call Ben names
Shouting after him 'Ben, don't you know you're thick?'
Ben would smile to himself, thinking little do they know
I don't miss a trick.

On a Wednesday Ben would go to the market
Arriving there when they were just packing up for the day,
They would fill his bag with over-ripe fruit
Ben thanked them then went happily on his way.

On fine nights Ben would sleep under a hedge
With a blanket to keep himself warm,
He would have a rain sheet with him
In case it rained or if there was a storm.

Sometimes when I am in my warm bed at night
I think of Ben somewhere out there,
It would be silly to worry about Old Ben though
Because he simply doesn't have a care.

Ena Page

SMILING EYES

It's his smile I remember most -
    not from his lips but from his eyes.
Like a teasing child, expectant -
    and quick to tantalise.
Remember how I had to guess,
    what was in the hand held out to me,
Nothing precious, just a little something
    you wanted me to see.
As I tried to think what your
    outstretched fingers held within
Our eyes would meet and laughingly
    our game would then begin
'Oh! Tell me, tell me
    just what you have found,
Is it blue or green -
    is it square or round?'
It didn't matter anyway -
    in my heart I had the prize -
The ever-present memory
    of those smiling, smiling eyes.

Margaret Pethers

A FRIEND

I never knew till you had gone
Just how much you'd meant to me
You were always there besides us,
We thought forever you'd be
There to share a laugh - a joke,
And have a cup o' tea.

You didn't say much, but you often sighed
Your thoughts in a special place.
You carried on with your struggle
And put on the bravest face.

I knew your sorrows and your joys
Your ups and downs I knew,
But could I ever understand
What loneliness you went through.

Perhaps I saw you as a mother,
Or more than just a friend
Perhaps a little of both I think
'Tis sad it all did end.

Parties, get-togethers, family do's
You said, 'Yes' to every call
We always tried to involve you,
And you always loved them all.

Then suddenly you've ceased to be
Within my daily view
No more I see you passing
No more I see of you.

My last memory I'll always keep
You were lovely to know
And I'll always see your smile face
Because you're on my video.

Winnie Milnes

MY DEAREST SIS

(Dedicated to my one and only big sister and best friend, Indresh)

Who cracks a joke a day?
Always annoying in every possible way.

The one who throws her books about?
Giving the most silliest looks around.

The one who is full of surprises
Obviously shows in her twinkling eyes.

She cares a lot about her surroundings
But when she is at home she does a lot of pounding.

Even though a lot goes on with her
I can't help loving her very much.

Niresha Umaichelvam (9)